The Prodigal Letters

Hannah Zhao

BookLeaf Publishing

Presentation by *BookLeaf Publishing*

Web: www.bookleafpub.com

E-mail: info@bookleafpub.com

ISBN: 9789358368932

First edition 2023

DEDICATION

This book is dedicated to my one and only Lord
and Savior, Jesus Christ!

ACKNOWLEDGEMENT

Where do I begin? Writing this book was truly the wildest journey...an unforgettable month filled with late nights and breakdowns...

The deepest thanks to my mom for always being there for me, offering me her shoulder to cry on, and being my #1 fan from day one.

A huge thank you to my sister Catherine for always being eager to read my writing, and especially for being willing to do my chores for me, without complaint, and love me, despite my moody breakdowns, during this crazy past month. I really can't thank you enough, Catherine!

Thank you so much to my dad for being so supportive and for always being so willing to patiently review my writing.

A warm thank you to Maya Adenihun, who first shared this poetry challenge with me.

Thank you to everyone who prayed for me throughout this challenge and especially when I struggled the most to reach the finish line.

Thank you, Holy Spirit, for giving me heavenly inspiration in your perfect timing!

And last but not least, thank you God for granting me this opportunity to grow and

express my faith, and ultimately, to glorify Your
Name!

PREFACE

"But while he was still a long way off, his father saw him and was filled with compassion for him; he ran to his son, threw his arms around him and kissed him. The son said to him, 'Father, I have sinned against heaven and against you. I am no longer worthy to be called your son.'

But the father said to his servants, 'Quick! Bring the best robe and put it on him. Put a ring on his finger and sandals on his feet. Bring the fattened calf and kill it. Let's have a feast and celebrate. For this son of mine was dead and is alive again; he was lost and is found.'"

Luke 15:20-24 NIV

Summer

The summer twilight is rich
With the aroma of wild honey
And succulent melons ripening
As a mellow breeze twirls through the fields.
There, in the distance underneath
An indigo sky, you come running
To me, little baby feet kissing
The warm earth, into my open arms.
Laughing, your Father kisses your
Rosy, dirt-stained cheeks, your flawless
Beauty, my child; the melody
Of your young heartbeat plays against
My chest as I carry you home, where
I cradle you in my arms and listen
To the soft murmur of your breathing as
Nearby, a chorus of crickets sing the warm night
away.

Home Sweet Home

Heavenly aroma of homemade
Food on a Sunday afternoon,
Loving embrace of mother's
Arms, marimba laughter
Of children playing
In golden bliss:
Fullness of
Home sweet
Home.

A Flame That Dies

3

At dawn the sun ignites the sky in flame;
As the day wakes, clouds skip across blue skies
Like smoke rings around alabaster flames
That dwindle to orange embers at dusk
And perish with thieving night:
For every day is but a flame that dies.

Autumn

The autumn morning glows gray;
The zephyr brings tidings
Of a distant storm as I stand
By the quiet roadside. The earth
Is damp from the remaining tears
Of the night: sandpaper leaves,
Drained of color, sag under the weight
Of crystal droplets of dew.

I watch as one by one, crumpled
Leaves bearing forgotten memories,
Fall without a whisper to their grave,
Buried in a rotting cemetery
Underneath ghostly, skeletal trees.
There, stamped into the debris, scattered
Down the forest path, are footprints.
Your footprints.

But this time, my child, you had not
Wandered off to splash in muddy puddles
Underneath indigo skies.
This time, my child, you had not
Wandered off to sing with the crickets
On a summer's eve.
This time, you ran away from home—

From me.

Home, which had, until now, felt like
The embrace of a warm bonfire
Crackling in the dark of night,
Feels suddenly cold, empty. Without you,
Everything seems to lose its luster.
A faded silver sky, rusted copper leaves,
Lost blue of the sky. Lost blush of
Rosy cheeks that once belonged to you.

Candles

If each life was a candle,
The world would be a giant flower of flame.
The Reaper holds the flower in His hands
And blows out the candles, one by one,
With gentle breath. The flower still shines,
fragile.

Yet how easy would it be for the Reaper
To blow the tiny flames all out at once,
To extinguish the light of the flower
With one final, terminating breath,
When the time of harvest finally comes?

The Eye of the Poet

There is a hollowness
In the poet's eyes,
A deep emptiness
Beneath a light that dies.

The poet's eyes are twin bolts of lightning,
The striking electric blue flashing
In a thunderstorm, like the frightening
Roar of heaven's armies clashing.

A war rages inside the poet's eyes.
Beneath the crystal blue lies a storm split
By jagged lightning and thunder cries
As clouds shed tears across a sky twilit.

But even as the clouds released
Their burden upon the ashen earth,
The storm is still not appeased,
Raging on for all it is worth.

The storm haunts the poet's eyes, for
It saw no rainbow echoing promise
And tasted no perfume of petrichor.
The poet's eyes reflect a grim illness.

Buried beneath those blue eyes of youth

Is the callow innocence of childhood
Sunken into the grave of naked truth.
The poet drinks the chalice of wormwood.

Buried beneath the lapis lazuli
Is hope with a stone rolled over its grave.
The poet is chained by the memory
Of the storm that made the poet its slave.

Still the poet birthed words onto a wordless
page.

Underneath a song of liberty
Is a captive soul;
Underneath a song of hope
Is a caged spirit, hopeless.

There is a hollowness
In the poet's eyes,
A deep emptiness
Beneath a light that dies.

The poet's eyes are the raw ice blue
Of a blizzard trapped by the darkness
Of the dawning night, as the wind blew
Snow across a moon-speckled wilderness.

But was there a moon?
On that snowy night,

Was there any moon?
Was there any light?

Or was the moon a trick of the light—
Or rather a trick of the darkness?
For the moon was swallowed that snowy night
By the blizzard that plagued the wilderness.

The poet's eyes are lit by the fragile
Light of the moon, the solitary light
In a dark complexion marked by futile
Hopes and dreams that died on a starless night.

But one night there will be no moon. Then
Night will truly be called night. One day
The light that had waxed and waned flaxen
Will, like deceased flesh, decay and rot gray.

And one day the light in the poet's eye
That had waxed and waned flaxen, as pain
Ebbed his waning life away, will die
With the rest of his harrowed frame.

The poet's words died with him in his grave.

Underneath a song of liberty
Is a captive soul;
Underneath a song of life
Is a caged spirit, dead.

Winter

The blizzard came suddenly
Last night, cruelly, devouring
The fields in its icy appetite.
The road is frozen this morning:
Like a priceless stone buried
Underneath an ocean of sand,
Your footprints are forever buried
Underneath a sea of snow.

Painfully, I recall the moment
I had stood by the road and welcomed your
Gossamer steps and butterfly smile
Into my arms that indigo summer
Countless seasons ago.

Now my heart breaks
Knowing that my little butterfly
Has sold its precious wings,
Laid its body naked in the cold
Like a barren tree made a victim
Of the blizzard.

How I long to feel
Your heartbeat against mine again,
To hear the heartstrings I tuned

When you were an instrument in the womb
Play me a melody!

How I long to cradle
You in my arms again, rock you gently
To sleep, hold you so tenderly so that
You would feel the safest in my arms!

My precious child,
My little butterfly, my beautiful rose,
If only you would come home to me,
I would run to you with open arms
And hold you and never let you go;
I would mend your broken wings
And stitch rainbows onto them;
I would cure your withered petals
With the water of everlasting life
—if only you would come home.

The Carpenter

The Carpenter carved a forest of wood,
Hammered a graveyard of nails
Into corpses of trees, knowing
That one day soldiers clad in scarlet
Would carve Him into rotting wood,
Hammer rusting nails into the humble
Hands that had once held the hammer,
Bent over wood and stone.

The Carpenter shaped a mountain of stones,
Chiseled a cemetery of limestone, knowing
That one day soldiers clad in scarlet
Would pierce His carcass with spear of flint
Before a man with stone heart turned flesh
Would bury His own deceased flesh
In tomb of chiseled limestone.

The Carpenter healed people
With the same calloused hands
That had carved wood,
Hammered nails,
Shaped stone,
Chiseled limestone, knowing
That one day, these same callous people
Would nail Him to the tree.

He wiped away the tears
Of the same people He shed tears for,
That night in the garden.
His tears fell the same crimson hue
That he bled on that tree
The very next day.

That night, His heart fell
For the same carpenter who felled the tree
That hung Him the very next day.

That night, His heart beat
For the same soldiers who beat Him
Crimson the very next day.

That night, the Carpenter bled
As He knelt by stone and prayed.

His hands created life
Out of the same wood
That He died on.
The Carpenter died at the hands
Of His own creation:
Carved on wood,
Pierced by nail,
Buried by the stone hearts
That rolled the stone over His grave.

The Carpenter died to heal the broken heart;
He died to save the wandering soul.
Yet just as a wildfire may kill and grow the same forest,
The Carpenter lived to conquer wood and nail.

At dawn on the third day,
The Carpenter reached out the punctured hand
Which wood had splintered and nail had pierced
To the broken, wandering child,
Saying, "Be Healed."

The Third Day

15

Life rolled a stone over death's tomb;
Death died, and darkness with it,
In light of the third day.

The Cardinal

Clouds drip gray over damp brown earth,
Night falls dark over winter's birth.

The moon lays cold over the silent grave
Of life with a stone rolled over its cave.

Feathers of white whisper by,
Singing a wordless lullaby.

Stained brown buried underneath stainless
white,
As night dawns in its inky light.

Time is frozen in the ice,
Still as the whiteness that never dies.

Then day breaks over the sweet slumber
Of a world drowned in white stupor.

Flakes of ice dance a little melody,
Ethereal in their delicate symmetry.

A flash of scarlet: a noble cardinal
Perches on the branch of a tree skeletal…

A flash of crimson: a noble King
Pierced on the skeleton of a tree, dying.

A single speck of cardinal red
In a white wilderness dead…

A single drop of blood shed
For a world that bled.

A song of quivering wings,
Hope taken flight sings…

Of a world painted white as snow by a crimson
sacrifice of atonement,
Of the cardinal that broke the spell of winter
with the promise of an eternal covenant.

Wildflowers

Fragrance of springtime,
Wildflowers clothed in fleeting
Beauty; why worry?

But even flowers'
Pretty heads wither and die—
Ever forgotten.

Life is but the swift
Shedding of flower petals:
Shudder, fade, and die.

Spring

Like daffodils blossoming around
Gravestones in a cemetery, the first
Snowdrops bloom from pearls of ice
As life spills color onto a lifeless canvas.

A flash of color—
The first butterfly after the snow.
The frozen landscape melts
To crystal rivers of light as
Sunlight splashes over a lucid dream:
Gossamer wings shine in the radiance
Of the full color spectrum,
Blinking a million colors at once,
Like light in living form.

There, in the distance,
Dressed in rags and filth,
I see you coming.

Your body is embraced by pain.
Your wings are broken.
Your rose is withered.

Yet in my eyes,
You are the first ray of sunshine after

The crippling darkness of the winter,
The first blossom after the snow,
The first butterfly after a frozen trance.

My little butterfly has returned.

I run to you, overwhelmed by joy,
With open arms, before you fall
Into my eternal embrace.

I kiss your dirt-stained cheeks;
Though this time, it is colored
Not by roses but by the gleam
Of freshly fallen tears.

I hold you tight, remove your wings of dust,
And adorn you with wings of snow
Washed white by crimson blood.

As the heart of Life begins to beat again,
Awakening the world from the dead of winter,
I hear your heartbeat racing against mine
And call you my own…

Healed

21

Heart broken like a potsherd,
Ever running to the healing
Arms of the Shepherd.
Little lamb carried by His loving
Embrace, through the waves spitting foam
Down the seashore and back home.

Quiet

Quiet,
By the hillside,
Sitting with my Savior.
Just you and me.

Quiet,
We listen
To the whisper of the wind,
The murmur of meadow grass
Swaying in a slow waltz.

Quiet,
You lovingly embrace me.
As a father embraces his child
So do you hold me close.
Cradled in your arms,
Your love overwhelms me.

Quiet,
You wipe away my every tear,
Though no one was there
To wipe your tears when you bled
That night in the garden.
You never leave my side,
Though everyone you loved

Deserted you in your plight.

Quiet,
You take up my cross
When I am too weak to bear it.
You carry my burden upon your shoulders.
Oh Jesus, how many blows have you taken for
me?
How many words have I spoken to shame you?
How far have I strayed from your love?
How many times have I unknowingly said,
"Crucify Him!" in my pride?
And yet, Jesus, how many times have you
forgiven me, again and again.

Oh Jesus, how so very deeply you love me.

Quiet,
You laid down your life for me,
Without a word.
You thought only of me.
How can I ever repay you?

I can never.

So

Quiet,
I bow my head and cry to you.

I cry a melody of silent tears,
And you listen.
The sound of my tears is your favorite song.
Because it means that finally,
Finally, with you,
I am at peace.

Solitude

25

O what a gift is solitude, the essence
Of peace on a lonely hilltop underneath
An oak tree, fully soaking in the presence
Of the Creator, who speaks life into breath.

O what a gift is solitude, the beauty
Of a patient, waiting heart, the clarity
Of quiet streams winding through a verdant lea,
In which God whispers, "Come, rest your soul in
me."

There is an Artist

There is an Artist who inspired breath from
creature of dust,
Spoke a masterpiece into existence,
Breathing life into lifeless earth.

There is a Painter who spilled color over a
colorless expanse,
Sparked a world of darkness into radiance,
Breathing life into a lifeless canvas.

There is an Author who engraved words onto a
wordless story,
Sealed it with His blood, shed like ink on
parchment,
Breathing life into a lifeless page.

There is a Composer who orchestrates a song in
songless souls,
Sings a caged songbird into freedom,
Breathing life into a lifeless instrument.

There is a Potter who molds meaning into a
meaningless pot,
Shapes it into a vessel of purpose,
Breathing life into lifeless clay.

There is an Artist who names His creation
Precious,
And you are His work of art:
His canvas, His page,
His instrument, His clay,
Made by Him and made for Him,
Destined to be known and loved by Him.

Prodigal

In the womb of time and space,
Before existence was conceived,
When He birthed the universe
And hung the stars across the void
Like lanterns lit in a dark night,
The Creator thought of me.

The Creator thought of how
I would one day gaze into
The depths of a starry lake
And see His reflection in mine.
Like Creator, like creation.
Like Father, like child.

When He drew the line between
Sky and sea, split the vault,
Separated water from water,
Then splashed waves of dawn
Across a horizon ablaze,
The Creator treasured me.

The Creator treasured the moment
I would one day stare toward the skyline
And see His love like a painting before me,
Setting the horizon and my heart on fire.

The world could be made of diamonds
Yet I was the treasure that He died to save.

In my mother's womb,
He pieced together every part of my being.
He knit me together, shaped me.
When He traced the intricate curve of my
fingers,
And tuned the delicate rhythm of my heartbeat,
The Creator loved me.

The Creator loved me even when I hated Him,
Even when I ran away from His love.
When I was the prodigal child, He was still the
Father
Who treasured me too much to give me up.
When I was the orphan child, He was still the
Father
Who loved me too much to abandon me.

As the stars danced across the heavens
And the sun waltzed through the seasons,
As the wind raced around the earth
And the waves crashed against the seashore,
When I was lost in my rebellion,
My Father waited for me to come home.

My Creator saw my dismay, heard my heavy
steps,

He tasted my shame and felt my pain
Long before I reached that golden gate.
My Father came running to me with open arms
Before I fell into His eternal embrace—
I, the prodigal child, have come home.

When I Wake

When I wake up I see Your face
As You shower the meadows with grace,
I see Your smile at the dawn of day
As color invades a horizon gray—
The beauty of Your smile makes my heart race.

I taste Your faithfulness as You trace
Love in gold letters on a sky ablaze,
As You clothe the wildflowers with the day
When I wake.

I breathe in Your love as You raise
Me up at the break of day to chase
Your laugh in the song of the jay,
To smell Your perfume where the poppies sway,
To feel Your eternal embrace
When I wake.